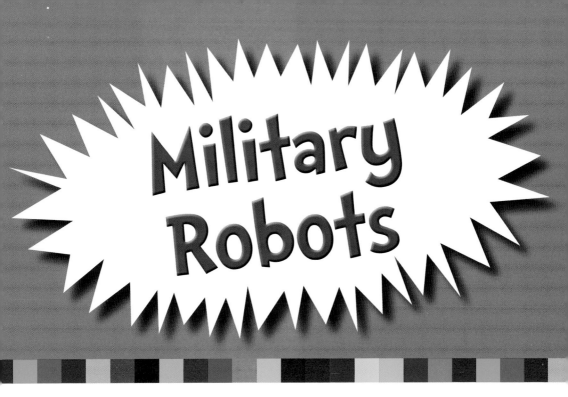

Military Robots

BY KIRSTEN W. LARSON

AMICUS HIGH INTEREST • AMICUS INK

Amicus High Interest and Amicus Ink are imprints of Amicus
P.O. Box 1329, Mankato, MN 56002
www.amicuspublishing.us

Library of Congress Cataloging-in-Publication Data
Names: Larson, Kirsten W., author.
Title: Military robots / by Kirsten W. Larson.
Description: Mankato, MN : Amicus High Interest, [2018] |
  Series: Robotics in our world | Includes index. | Audience:
  Grades 4-6.
Identifiers: LCCN 2016034048| ISBN 9781681511443
  (library binding) | ISBN 9781681521756 (pbk.) | ISBN
  9781681512341 (ebook)
Subjects: LCSH: Military robots–United States–Juvenile
  literature.
Classification: LCC UG450 .L37 2018 | DDC 623–dc23
LC record available at https://lccn.loc.gov/2016034048

Editor: Wendy Dieker
Series Designer: Kathleen Petelinsek
Book Designer: Tracy Myers
Photo Researcher: Holly Young

Photo Credits: U.S. Air Force/Staff Sgt. Samuel Morse/
Department of Defense cover; 2nd Marine Aircraft Wing
(FWD), Cpl. Justin M. Boling/WikiCommons 4-5; Sgt Anthony
Boocock, RLC/WikiCommons 6; Peter Macdiarmid/Getty
Images 9; Mary Evans / Sueddeutsche Zeitung Photo 10;
Francis Miller/The LIFE Picture Collection/Getty 13; Staff Sgt.
Samuel Morse/DVIDS 14; 121st Public Affairs Detachment,
Staff Sgt. Peter Morrison/WikiCommons 17; US Air Force
Photo/Alamy Stock Photo 18; Radharc Images/Alamy Stock
Photo 21; Associated Press/Yomiuri Shimbun 22; U.S. Navy
photo by John F. Williams/DVIDS 25; KIM DONG-JOO/AFP/
Getty Images 26; Stocktrek Images/Getty 28-29

Printed in the United States of America

HC 10 9 8 7 6 5 4 3 2 1
PB 10 9 8 7 6 5 4 3 2 1

Table of Contents

What Are Military Robots?

A helicopter buzzes along a line of mountains. It is in Afghanistan. It carries food, water, and other gear. These items will help American soldiers. It is time to land. Cameras scan for the perfect spot. Then the chopper lands. But wait! There is no pilot inside. How did this chopper land by itself? It is a robot.

A robot helicopter can take supplies from a military base to a camp with no pilot inside.

The chopper's computer tells it where to fly. The aircraft has **sensors**. They look for objects in the way. What if it spots another plane? No problem! The computer steers the chopper to safety.

Why does the military need a robot helicopter? It is safer. Carrying gear by truck is risky. Enemies often attack the **convoys**. They also shoot down aircraft. This way, no one gets hurt.

A group of trucks can be an easy target. It's dangerous for the drivers to move supplies.

Not all military robots fly. Some work
on land or at sea. Robots are used to
keep soldiers safe. Some do risky jobs like
destroying bombs. Others spy on enemies.
Some alert soldiers to danger. They find
mines in the ocean that could destroy ships.
Military robots help soldiers everywhere.
The role of robots is only growing.

A robot searches for bombs in a field. This job is very risky for people to do.

A Russian soldier stands next to a line of tanks in 1940.

 Who invented remote control?

The History of Military Robots

During World War I (1914-18), machine guns, planes, and tanks made war more deadly. Leaders needed to keep soldiers safe. One way was to keep soldiers off the battlefield. In 1940, Russian soldiers drove remote control **teletanks**. The drivers were a mile (1.6 km) away. The tanks carried guns and bombs. Boom!

 Nikola Tesla did. He designed a small, remote control boat in 1898. Forty years later, people drove full size tanks by remote control!

Teletanks were not true robots. People still had to tell them what to do. They would need computers to be robots. It didn't take long before computers were invented. In 1945, the ENIAC became the first electronic computer in the U.S. It did math calculations that took people days to finish. It could do 5,000 addition problems in one second. Amazing!

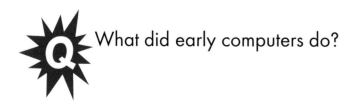 What did early computers do?

Women programed the ENIAC to do complex math. They helped the military do many jobs.

 One of their first jobs was cracking codes. These computers led to the invention of robots.

What Makes a Robot Work?

Robots need three things to work. They need a computer, sensors, and the ability to act. Take away one of these things, and there is no robot.

A robot's sensors work like eyes or ears. They take in information. This goes to the computer. It is the robot's brain. The brain is programed to tell the robot's parts how to move.

This robot has a camera for eyes. Its computer tells the tool to grab items it sees.

Today, many robots work mostly by remote control. Yet they can do some tasks on their own. The PackBot robot is one of these. It can spy. It also can find and take apart bombs. Soldiers drive it with game-like controllers or tablets. But the robot can drive itself if it needs to. What if it flips over? It can turn itself right side up again.

 What other jobs can a PackBot do?

Soldiers practice using a PackBot. The soldiers will later use the robot to find bombs in the field.

 It can sense harmful chemicals or **radiation**.

The *Predator* is called an unmanned aerial vehicle, or UAV. The pilot is not in the plane.

Where is the drone's pilot?

Pilots also fly drones like *Predator*. This robot drone spies on U.S. enemies in other countries. It can launch missiles too. **GPS** tells the plane where it is and where it needs to go. If *Predator* loses touch with its pilot, it circles and waits. It may fly home. An **autopilot** system steers the drone if a person cannot.

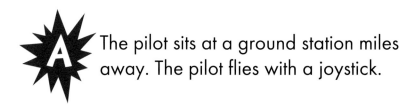

The pilot sits at a ground station miles away. The pilot flies with a joystick.

The U.S. Navy uses underwater drones to hunt for mines. They use **sonar**, or sound waves, for this job. The drone sends out sound waves. They bounce off objects on the seafloor making a picture. The drone compares the pictures with those stored in its computer memory. When it spots a mine, it lets the sailors know.

 Does someone drive the navy's sea drone?

A drone like this searches for mines underwater.

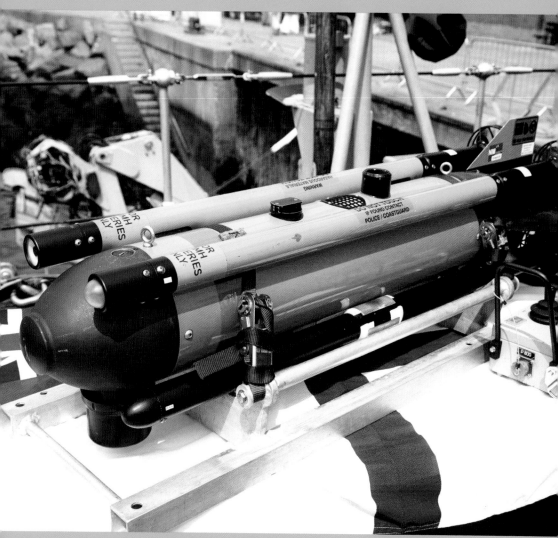

 No. It drives all by itself. People keep watch over it. They can take over if they need to.

The NASA research lab built this robot to compete in the DARPA robotics challenge in 2013.

What is DARPA?

What Comes Next?

Will lifelike robots march with soldiers someday? Maybe. But making them is hard. DARPA held an Olympic-like robot challenge. People built robots to do eight tasks. Robots moved through rubble. They climbed a ladder. Yet many robots tumbled. The fastest robot finished the course in 45 minutes. A person would have finished faster.

 It is the Defense Advanced Research Projects Agency. It works to develop new technology for the U.S. military.

Machines continue to do more and more on their own. In the future, robots might work totally without people. The U.S. Navy is testing the *Sea Hunter* ship. It steers all by itself. **Radar** and cameras help it spot objects in its way. Sailors on shore keep an eye on the ship by computer.

 Do people drive the *Sea Hunter*?

A ceremony marks the first day the *Sea Hunter* robotic ship takes to the ocean.

 No. It steers all by itself. During testing, a person is on board, ready to take over if something goes wrong.

A South Korean soldier helps show how the robot guard can find and stop people at the border.

Q How does South Korea use its robot guards?

Should robots fight instead of people in wars? People are not sure. Technology makes robot soldiers possible. But should we use them? Many people think only a person should give an order to kill. South Korea already has an armed robot guard. It has cameras and motion sensors. It watches for people and vehicles. A person can tell it to shoot.

 They are stationed along the border with North Korea, an enemy nation.

Robot Fighters

Military robots play a big role in today's wars. Robot helicopters carry gear. Robot planes spy. They drop bombs. On the ground, robots stand guard. At sea, they hunt for mines and enemy subs. As robot technology advances, their role may get bigger. Will they replace soldiers in battle? No one can say. It might happen one day.

This military robot finds bombs. What other jobs will it do in the future?

Glossary

autopilot A system for automatically controlling an airplane, ship, or spacecraft.

convoy A group of vehicles traveling together.

GPS Short for Global Positioning System; a network of satellites that sends information about a device's location on Earth.

mine An underwater or underground bomb.

radar A way ships and planes find objects; they send out radio waves, which bounce off the object and send the signal back.

radiation Rays of energy, such as light or heat; some kinds of radiation are harmful.

sensor An instrument that detects changes in something and responds by sending a signal.

sonar A way of sending sound waves to locate an object.

teletank A remote control tank; a person drives the tank using remote control from a safer place.

Read More

Clay, Kathryn. *Robots in Risky Jobs: On the Battlefield and Beyond.* North Mankato, Minn.: Capstone Press, 2014.

Stark, William N. *Mighty Military Robots.* Military Machines on Duty. North Mankato, Minn.: Capstone Press, 2016.

Stewart, Melissa. *Robots.* Washington, D.C.: National Geographic Children's Books, 2014.

Websites

Idaho Public Television Robotics
http://idahoptv.org/sciencetrek/topics/robots/index.cfm

Kids Discover: Drones to the Rescue
http://www.kidsdiscover.com/teacherresources/drones-uavs-rescue/

Science Kids: Robots for Kids
http://sciencekids.co.nz/robots.html

Index

About the Author

Kirsten W. Larson is the author of more than 20 books for young readers. She used to work with rocket scientists at NASA, but now she writes about science for kids. Her favorite robots are NASA's *Curiosity* Mars Rover and LEGO Mindstorms. She lives near Los Angeles, California. Learn more at kirsten-w-larson.com.